Alnwick in the Gı

CW00540141

Stories from the Hom
Alnwick and District

Contents

Wanney Books

www.wildsofwanney.co.uk

Foreword

For most of us, the Great War evokes images of the trenches of France and Belgium, with the soldiers braving a hail of machine gun fire as they "go over the top". This view has been partly created by the literature that we have of this period, from the War Poets to books such as "Goodbye to All That" and "Birdsong".

The terrible losses during the four years of war continue to cast a shadow over our nation. The memorials to the dead and missing that have been erected in every town and village provide an ongoing reminder to us all of the ultimate sacrifice that our armed forces are asked to give on our behalf. But while the war in the trenches must have been a horrific experience, the conflict was much broader than that.

The Great War marked a major change in the life of all British people. It was the first conflict that involved everyone in the land and as a result It changed the face of Britain. The country that existed in 1914 would disappear forever and it has been said that modern Britain, as we know it today, began to emerge in 1918.

So what did the Great War mean to people on the home front? In this small book I will try to tell some of the inter-related stories about how the war was experienced in and around Alnwick, a small market town in one of the more remote parts of England. And although the stories may be about the Alnwick district, they will probably have a resonance for people in many small towns through the length and breadth of Britain.

The stories are not complete. There are still many gaps to be filled, but the book will hopefully tell some interesting tales and may act as a spur for others to continue the research.

Ian Hall - July 2014

NOTE: The book includes quotes from contemporary documents. These are shown in italics. I have made no attempt to correct any spellings in these sections but have included notes within square brackets as clarification.

The Outbreak of War

The declaration of war on 4th August 1914 was met with a general wave of popular patriotism. Almost immediately the whole country became involved in the war effort. The prevailing view was that we would go over and sort out the Germans, and all be home for Christmas. As we now know, things turned out a little differently!

Once war had been declared, the Army was quickly despatched to the continent to link up with the French in order to repulse the advancing German forces. Known as the British Expeditionary Force, it comprised almost the whole of the home-based Regular Army as it existed at the start of the war.

At the same time as the Regular Army was being sent to France, the Territorial Army[1] was being mobilised. The Territorials were originally supposed to be for home defence only, but the needs of the Army on the continent meant that most would now serve overseas.

The local Territorials were the 7th Battalion Northumberland Fusiliers (7th NF). In Alnwick they met and trained in the Drill Hall on Fenkle Street [image 5].

As well as mobilising the Regulars and Territorials, there was also an urgent drive to recruit more soldiers. Within a week of the outbreak of war, notices appeared in the the local paper announcing that the recruiting station at Alnwick Town Hall would be open from 9.00am each day.

The volunteers from Alnwick and other towns in the area were mainly enlisted into the 7th NF Territoral Battalion. The new recruits were billeted in Alnwick until a sufficient number of men had been gathered, when they were then sent by train to the battalion training camp that had been established at Gosforth Park [1].

---

[1] In the years running up to 1914 the Territorials was a popular activity for young men; in the days before paid work holidays, the opportunity for an annual camp in the country, with pay, must have made volunteering very attractive.

The Alnwick and County Gazette (A&C Gazette) reported on 19th September 1914:

About one hundred and twenty recruits, including several men who had seen service, and who had been undergoing a short period of training, were despatched to join the 7th Battalion Northumberland Fusiliers at present lying at Gosforth Park and Byker. They left the Drill Hall in Fenkle Street fully equipped, and they were played to the railway station[2] by a section of the drum and fife band, being followed by a large and patriotic crowd of the towns people.

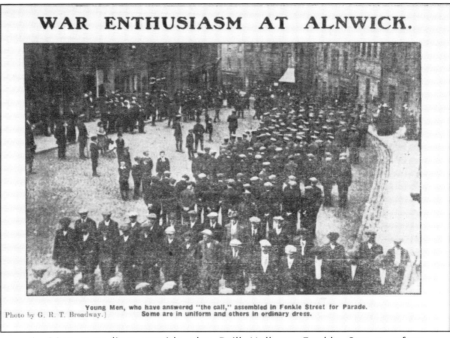

1: Men parading outside the Drill Hall on Fenkle Street, after enlisting into the Army

During the winter of 1914 the Gosforth Park camp became a quagmire and the soldiers were moved into billets at Cambois, later returning to Gosforth Park. In March 1915 they went to Belgium as part of the Northumberland Infantry

---

[2] The railway station is now occupied by Barter Books and others

Brigade. They played a key role in the second battle of Ypres in April 1915, assisting in preventing a German breakthrough.

While the military was being mobilised and expanded, what we would now call "civil defence" was also being organised. The A&C Gazette reported in its 8th August edition:

> *The four special constables in Alnwick have got notice to be in readiness for duty.*

The history of the Special Constabulary (the Specials) goes back to the days of Charles II, when an act was passed that allowed ordinary citizens to be sworn in as temporary peace-officers if there was a threat of major disorder. Over the years the scope and authority of this body was increased, and it became known as the Special Police. Up until WW1, however, they were still only called upon in times of need to augment the Police Force, with only a token skeleton force retained between times. On the outbreak of war, the announcement in the local paper shows this force being brought to readiness.

Locally the Special Constabulary was the responsibility of the Chief Constable, who was based in Morpeth. Very quickly, more local men were being sworn in as Special Constables and an organisation was being established, based on Petty Sessional boundaries. These were the basis of the magistrate courts at that time. Alnwick's Specials became the East Coquetdale Ward Petty Sessional Division and were initially organised as follows:

- No 1 Group—Lesbury; Group Leader: Thomas Reavell
- No 2 Group—Alnwick South; Group Leader: Marcus Wade
- No 3 Group—Denwick; Group leader: Robert Middlemas
- No 4 Group—Alnwick North; Group Leader: Hugh Archbold
- No 5 Group—Alnmouth and Shilbottle; Group leader: Hugh Percy

The Special Constables were all issued with a badge, but no uniform. They were not to carry fire arms and were considered non-combatant.

Initially, the Specials had little to do, apart from assisting the Police in some duties. In October 1914, the Chief Constable wrote to all the Group leaders asking them to be wary of hay stack fires. There is also a hint of a fear of subversive activities in his letter.

> *When these fires are not accidental, the perpetrator is very difficult to discover and the presence and assistance of the Special Constable will therefore be all the more welcome.*

As well as recruiting for the Army and mobilising the Special Constabulary, there was a rush of other activities to support the war effort. Everybody wanted to be involved in some way.

Boys were recruited into a messenger service. The local paper reported that Boy Scouts and Church Lads Brigade provided a team of 18 "fine healthy boys" within the first few weeks of war. It is unclear whether the messenger service was ever used.

On 17th August, the Duke of Northumberland hosted a public meeting at the Corn Exchange where he launched the Lord Lieutenant's War Fund. In the days before any significant state funded welfare system, this fund would have helped to relieve some of the distress caused by the war. The fund grew quickly. By 29th August it amounted to £42,759, and it continued to rise in subsequent months. The A&C Gazette reported weekly on all subscriptions, however small.

Hospitals were also prepared for injured soldiers. Local ladies volunteered for nursing duties. They were known as Voluntary Aid Detachments (VAD) and were organised by the Red Cross.

Lady Victoria Percy, one of the Duke's daughters, organised the local VAD, establishing a hospital in the Duchess's School on Bailiffgate. This opened in January 1915 as the 8th Northumberland V.A.D. Hospital. Locally there was another hospital, the 1st Northumberland V.A.D. Hospital, at Howick Hall.

Meanwhile, on the outbreak of war, three German ships were lying in Amble harbour. These were impounded and later sold. The German sailors who were on board at the time were held in the Alnwick workhouse[3] until November 1914 when they were sent to an internment camp at Wakefield for the remainder of the war.

So we see, in the first few weeks of the war, the local population becoming engaged in the war effort. As the conflict progressed we will see how much more the war would impact on the local population.

Getting the news

Throughout the war, people would be kept informed mainly through newspapers, both national and local; there were of course no radios. The local paper was the Alnwick and County Gazette, which was published weekly throughout the war.

In 1914, each edition of the paper had eight pages, with the first two almost entirely put over to advertisements; local businesses on the front page and classifieds inside. There were no headlines as we know them today. The content was reasonably standard for the first few years, covering such items as Council News, Angling Notes, Auction Marts and Sales and The Garden This Week. Increasingly we see Alnwick and District War News in the newspaper which provided both national and local war news.

By 1917 the paper was down to four pages, with nearly half of this still dedicated to advertisements. In 1918 we see a two page War Supplement being issued, which included photographs and cartoons.

Alongside the newspaper, the cinema in the Corn Exchange[4] would sometimes show patriotic news films from the Front.

---

[3] The Alnwick workhouse was housed in the building near the bottom of Waggonway Road which today is the Citizens Advice Bureau.

[4] The Corn Exchange is at the top of some steps that lead up from Bondgate Within. It is destined to be a Wetherspoons pub.

The Spectre of Invasion

In 2009 a series of papers was discovered in an auction lot in Liverpool. These were found to refer to the little-known invasion precautions that were implemented in the Alnwick area, mainly during 1914 and 1915. The papers were offered by their new owner, Kevin Barron, to the North Northumberland Branch of the Western Front Association and this is the first opportunity for the contents to be brought to wider public attention.

By October 1914, open warfare had ground to a halt and a line of trenches was being established from the Belgian coast to Switzerland. It was becoming apparent that the war would not be over by Christmas; indeed the likelihood was that the war would now last for a long time. This raised the age-old fear of invasion.

While it might seem unlikely that the Germans would choose the Northumberland coast as their landing site, the coastal defences further south might well have made this area a more attractive landing area.

In order to organise the country to face up to this threat of invasion, Local Emergency Committees (LEC) were established throughout Britain. As with the Special Constabulary, they were based on the Petty Sessional boundaries.

The organisation for Northumberland was established on 9th November 1914, at a meeting hosted by the Duke of Northumberland, acting in his role as Lord Lieutenant of the county. The East Coquetdale LEC was to be chaired by Arthur Scholefield[5]. The day following this meeting, he was writing, inviting people to join the LEC [2].

Nationally, a framework for invasion precautions was developed and a "secret" document was issued on 17th November 1914 which gave more detail into what preparations were considered necessary. This would provide the basis for the work of the LEC and Special Constables for the remainder of the war.

The following is an abridged version of that document:

---

[5] Arthur Scholefield was a ship owner as well as a director of a number of major companies. After his marriage in 1883 he built his house, Lint Close, in Alnmouth. This is now the Friary.

Lint Close,
Alnmouth,
Northumberland.

Nov. 10th. 1914.

Confidential.

Dear Sir,

PREPARATIONS FOR ACTION IN THE EVENT OF INVASION.

I have been appointed Chairman for the District comprised within the last Coquetdale Petty Sessions, and at a Meeting held in the Moot Hall yesterday at which the Lord Lieutenant, the Duke of Northumberland, presided, Committees were formed for the divisions of the County.

Your name was selected as one of those to act on my Committee.

I hope shortly to be supplied with Ordnance Maps and printed instructions as to arrangements which have to be made. We must arrange later on the place and time that would be most convenient but to begin with I shall be glad if you would come to my House at three o'clock on Saturday afternoon the 14th. inst.. We then could have a general discussion on the whole project.

Yours faithfully,

Arthur Scholefield.

If you have any useful maps perhaps you would be good enough to bring them with you.

Admiral Baker Baker,

Lesbury.

2: One of the letters sent by Arthur Scholefield, informing the recipient of their involvement in the Local Emergency Committee

1. *To submit to the Chief Constable the names of suitable men for appointment as Special Constables.*

2. *To organise a Cycle Despatch Corps to be attached to the Group Leaders of the Special Constables for the transmission of orders*

3. *To advise the Central Organising Committee of suitable collecting areas for transport animals and light carts*

4. *Cattle removal and destruction: Instructions will be given by the military representative on the Committee.*

5. *To advise the Central Organising Committee of suitable collecting places [for motors and bicycles], to register the names and addresses of owners and to instruct them to render useless for transport any vehicles left behind.*

6. *On receipt of order to collect entrenching tools, barbed and other wire, wire netting, and anything useful for blocking roads, or for military field works.*

7. *To register the names of labourers available to assist the military in making entrenchments and earth works.*

8. *To give all assistance to our own Supply Officers if called upon to assist in collecting supplies that may be required for our troops.*

9. *To arrange for the removal or destruction of stores of Petrol, [and] Rubber Tyres.*

10. *To arrange for the removal or destruction of such Boats, Barges, and Rafts as may be indicated by the Central Organising Committee.*

11. *To arrange for posting two or more Special Constables at important cross roads, to keep roads clear for the military, and to direct them and the civil population as required.*

12. *To do everything possible to keep the inhabitants from encumbering the roads required by the Military Authorities.*

From this point, the plans began to develop very quickly. On 25th November the Chief Constable wrote to all Group Leaders, requesting that they start gathering information on:

> vehicles, horses, motors, petrol stores, flour supplies etc. and imagine a movement being ordered to the west and how it would best work out as an orderly exodus and not as a stampede

and to:

> talk quietly to the farmers when he is going about and prepare the way for such an exodus not coming as a shock (if it ever does come) but rather as a thing which has been quietly thought out and arranged for.

On the 1st December 1914 Arthur Scholefield was able to report that arrangements for the receiving of stock and vehicles from Alnwick district had been agreed with Mr Clayhills, the Chairman of the neighbouring North Coquetdale LEC.

Stock would enter the North Coquetdale area at Lemmington Bank Top, Shipley Lane End, Eglingham and Old Bewick, from where it would be deposited in the Breamish and Alnham valleys. Motors would be transferred to Ingram, Alnham and Thrunton Wood sawmill.

The organisation of the evacuation of stock continued through the winter, with Group Leaders collating the numbers of cattle and sheep that would be moving from each farm. By 23rd February 1915, Mr Clayhills was able to advise his own Group Leaders where the stock from the Alnwick area would be relocated to. We can see that 4,711 cattle and 33,573 sheep were planned to be moved.

Meanwhile, on 18th December 1914, the Chief Constable was proposing a method of coordinating all the various evacuation routes in order to ensure the effectiveness of the whole operation. He proposed that Route Books be created that would describe the roads that would be used for the evacuation and he provided examples of books that had already been prepared in Lincolnshire. The Chief Constable made the following particular point:

A careful comparison of the roads as marked on the maps supplied will be necessary so that each road may get its fair share of the traffic and so the chance of congestion is minimised.

As a result, two main evacuation routes were adopted which would lead to the North Coquetdale area. Local evacuation routes would join these two main routes at convenient points and Special Constables would man junctions to direct the flow of people, vehicles and stock.

The northerly route led from the coast near Boulmer to the Eglingham road, via Denwick, using minor roads and tracks.

The southerly route led from the coast south of the Aln estuary to Lemmington Bank Top, via Shilbottle. This route used a short part of the Great North Road, but Special Constables and others would be on hand to ensure any evacuation didn't clash with military traffic moving north to engage with the enemy.

The Specials continued with the job of quantifying what would be involved in an evacuation. The lists of stock had been completed, but there was now a need for lists of vehicles, food, fuel, spades, wire and shotguns, as well as men who were willing to help the military if required [3].

In Alnmouth, it was recorded that the various shops had over six tons of tinned goods, nearly five tons of other food stuffs and about 400 gallons of oil; a considerable amount for a small village.

Park Farm within Hulne Park was declaring that they had the following materials available:

22 ordinary spades, 4 draining spades, 25 shovels, 4 pick axes, 2 axes, 8 hand saws, 1 cross cut saw, 250 yards of fencing wire and 200 yards of sheep netting

In early December each Group Leader compiled a brief status report on his area and followed up with a more detailed report around Christmas time. These reports were sent to Mr Middlemas, who may now have been acting as the deputy to Arthur Scholefield.

On 24th December 1914, Marcus Wade, the Group Leader for Alnwick South, was able to make the following report:

Removal of Cattle and Farm Stock; Messrs W Robinson, J Sordy and R Rickaby have been appointed to direct and see that this is properly carried out.

Cycle Despatch Corps; Messrs J Purvis, J Fairbairn, W Hudson, A H Hare and Frank Wallace.

Cross Roads; The following will be stationed as under:

Lemmington Bank	*G Brown*
Mossy Ford Bridge	*W Young*
Clayport Top	*W Bell*
Royal Oak	*J Armstrong*
Rugley Road End	*J D Thompson*
Hadwins Close	*Harry Forster*

whose duties will be to direct all animals, transport vehicles, inhabitants and military.

The Town: That portion of the town within my area has been sub-divided into blocks running south as under at which the following members are stationed:

Clayport Top to St Michael's Lane	*James Gray*
Clayport Prudhoe Road End	*D T Castles*
St Michael's Lane to Hotspur Tower	*T Forster*
Hotspur Tower to the Railway Station	*T Cunningham*
New Buildings	*R Holt*
Railway Station to Royal Oak	*E Croudace*
Royal Oak to Alndyke	*A Smith*

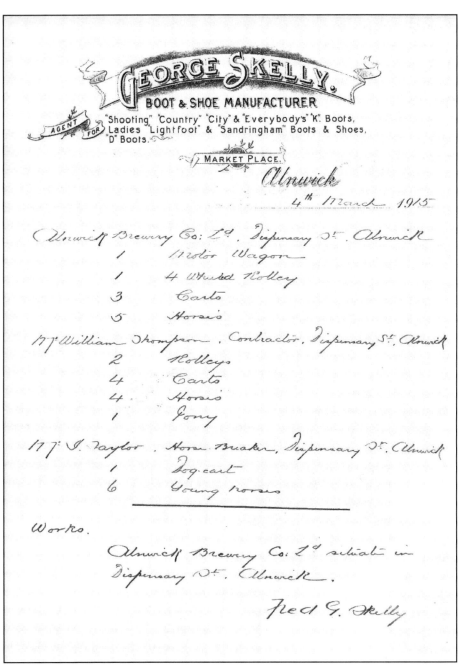

GEORGE SKELLY.

BOOT & SHOE MANUFACTURER

"Shooting" "Country" "City" & "Everybody's" "K". Boots,
Ladies "Lightfoot" & "Sandringham" Boots & Shoes,
"D" Boots.

AGENT FOR

MARKET PLACE.

Alnwick

4th March 1915

Alnwick Brewery Co: Ld, Dispensary St. Alnwick

1	Motor Wagon
1	4 Wheeled Rolley
3	Carts
5	Horse's

Mr William Thompson, Contractor, Dispensary St. Alnwick

2	Rolleys
4	Carts
4	Horse's
1	Pony

Mr J. Taylor, Horse Breaker, Dispensary St. Alnwick

1	Dog-cart
6	Young horses

Works.

Alnwick Brewery Co: Ld situate in
Dispensary St. Alnwick.

Fred G. Skelly

3: One of the lists of vehicles that was prepared by the Special
Constables. Fred Skelly was a member of the Alnwick North Group.

whose duties will be to see to the removal of all animals, transport vehicles, bicycles, barbed wire, entrenching tools etc. and the direction of the inhabitants.

Rendezvous; On the alarm being given all the members (with the exception of Messrs Robinson, Sordy, Rickaby, G Brown and Frank Wallace) will assemble at the Police Station to receive final instructions before taking up their stations.

With reference to:

Messrs Robinson, Sordy and Rickaby a dispatch rider will be sent to warn them to act.

G Brown is to proceed without delay to his station at Lemmington Bank Top.

Frank Wallace has his instructions in the event of the alarm occurring during the night time to proceed with all despatch on his motor cycle to Edlingham Station and warn the station master to make immediate preparations for the running of trains from Alnwick.

Plans were also being prepared for the evacuation of civilians to Wooler. On the 21st December, the North East Railway confirmed the arrangements:

Referring to the conversation of date, to transfer the people of Alnwick to Wooler between the hours of 8.[00]pm and 7.50am it would be necessary to send messengers by road on motor car or bike to all level crossings and stations up to Wooler to open the branch and give particulars of train services as far as possible.

During the day a train could be worked every two hours but if more vehicles and locomotives were available trains could be worked more frequently and arrangements made to pass at Whittingham.

We usually have 35 passenger vehicles here at the weekend and overnight, but during the day 20 or more are in use for ordinary trains. We frequently have 20 or more cattle trucks also and those in case of great emergency could be utilised.

June 24th 1915.

Alnwick

Special Constables - Despatch Riders Test.

The Despatch Rider must call at each of the places mentioned below, and to shew that he has called at each place, the signature of a responsible person must be obtained.

William T. Meech

Group Leader.

Name of Place.	Signature.
1. Broom House Farm.	*A. Little*
2. High House Farm.	*Wm Bolton*
3. Shipley Farm.	*R. Noble*
4. Bannamoor Farm.	*J. Rogerson*
5. Friars Well.	*H. Geggie*
6. Hulne Abbey.	*Tom Meech*
7. Park Farm.	*John Potter*
8. Park Saw Mills.	*no occupant at present*

Left 6-30 P.m.
Returned 7-55 P.m.
Completed in
1 hr 25 minutes
William T. Meech
Group Leader

Mr. Robert Miller,

Special Constable.

no 248

4: A record of one of the Cycle Desptach Rider tests that were carried out during July 1915. William Meech was Group Leader for the Hulne Park Group, created after the initial organisation was established.

16

By the end of the year, the overall plans were sufficiently clear for the Duke of Northumberland to prepare a printed proclamation, titled

Instruction for the Guidance of the Civil Population in the Event of a Landing by the Enemy in this Country

This was professionally printed in Newcastle and was dated 25th January 1915. It is unclear, however, whether this was ever made public. There does not seem to have been any mention of it in the local newspaper and on 24th January, Arthur Scholefield wrote to Mr Middlemas to say that:

the Duke thought the instructions as to food, blankets etc. should come from the Group Leaders and not by Proclamation.

There had already been indications that there was an element of secrecy about the invasion planning. Previously, on 8th December 1914, Arthur Scholefield had written:

I tried hard to get permission for our instructions to be printed and circulated but after full consideration the Military representatives declined to allow this, and finally it was agreed that the Committees might issue written instructions to Special Constables who in turn were only to give verbal instructions.

By the middle of 1915 the Cycle Despatch Corps was well established and tests of the speed and effectiveness of this method of communication were being carried out. The riders had to visit a series of farms, obtaining a signature on a card at each, and then return to the Police station [4].

On the 6th July 1915, Thomas Reavell, the Group Leader for Lesbury, was able to report to Mr Middlemas that the eight farms in his district had been visited in a time of 55 minutes by two motor cyclists.

We are now getting towards the end of the LEC story as we know it. On 26th August 1915 Arthur Scholefield wrote to Mr Middlemas:

I shall this morning send instructions for a "test" to be made the same day, and this will be based on the assumption that hostile transports have left their base and may land anywhere on the East Coast.

The test will apply merely to Live Stock, Cross Roads, etc. just as in the trials, and not to the Civil Population.

There are no records to show that such a test was carried out, and as there is no mention in the local papers, at the moment we have a mystery.

The documentation relating to the Local Emergency Committee now dries up.

Arthur Scholefield was seconded to a Board of Trade committee which would require him to be in London for one week in two. On 8th November he wrote to Mr Middlemas to inform him of this and that he would therefore not be able to continue with his role for the coming winter. He then seems to hand over the LEC leadership to Mr Middlemas.

The spectre of invasion did not, however, diminish. The Royal Flying Corps who, by 1916, were operating in the Alnwick area, countering the threat of Zeppelin raids, were expected to provide support in case of an attempted invasion. This would have included reconnaissance, bombing of hostile transports and cooperation with infantry on the ground, in line with what the RFC was doing on the Western Front.

So although we currently have no records, we can assume that the invasion precautions continued for much of the remainder of the war, with the Specials taking a central role.

One result of the Specials being so involved in helping to protect the civilian population was that after the war, legislation was enacted to maintain them as a permanent body, providing unpaid assistance to the regular Police. This situation has continued to the present day.

5: The Drill Hall on Fenkle Street today. Originally a bank, it was purchased in 1866 by the Duke of Northumberland for the use of local militia.

6: The remains of rifle range target butts at Moorlaws (OS map reference NU143137). It is unclear whether all of these remains are from the period of the Great War.

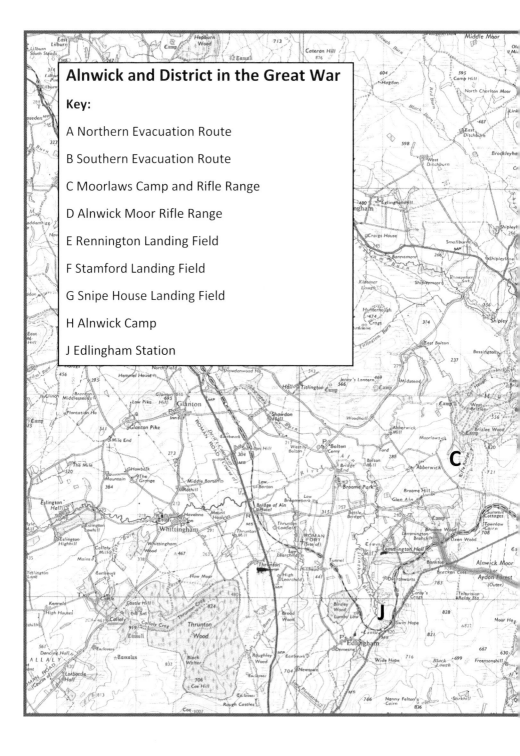

Alnwick and District in the Great War

Key:

A Northern Evacuation Route

B Southern Evacuation Route

C Moorlaws Camp and Rifle Range

D Alnwick Moor Rifle Range

E Rennington Landing Field

F Stamford Landing Field

G Snipe House Landing Field

H Alnwick Camp

J Edlingham Station

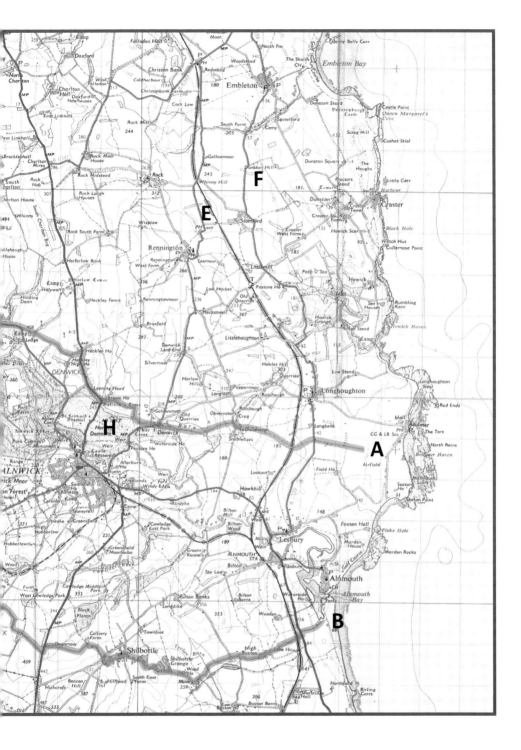

7: Soldiers who died in the UK were usually buried close to their home. These are three of the soldiers' graves in the Alnwick cemetery.

8: A view of the North Road entrance into the Alnwick camp today. This part of the pastures is not normally open to the public.

The Army in Alnwick

On 5th August 1914, the day after war was declared, a detachment of the Northern Cyclists Battalion arrived in Alnwick to provide for local defence. They were billeted in and around the town, using Green Batt House as their officers' mess.

The Cyclist Battalions were Territorials and had been formed prior to 1914 to provide for reconnaissance and communications, though they were equipped as infantry. Locally they would have been expected to respond to any invasion attempt, prior to the arrival of reinforcements.

At the same time, recruits for the 7th NF stayed in the locality until there were a sufficient number to be transferred to other, more advanced, training areas. The local paper reported in October 1914 that:

> *several hundreds of young patriots who remain billeted in the town are daily and enthusiastically fitting themselves for the grim art of war. They have been regularly put through athletic exercises and drill formations, with a route march now and again. They are now being instructed in musketry and have practice at the Stobby Moor and Moor Laws ranges.*

While they were waiting in Alnwick, these new soldiers were not just trained in military subjects. In the evenings:

> *French lessons are being given to the soldiers remaining in Alnwick in the New Parish Hall. The two lessons already given have been largely attended. Lady Margaret Percy* [another of the Duke's daughters] *has very kindly undertaken to conduct the lessons.*

Across the country, men were being recruited into Kitchener's New Army. These new units were often formed on the "pals" principle, where men who lived or worked together would be recruited into the same regiment. This was intended to ease the new recruits transition into Army life, but it had the unintended consequence of leaving whole communities devastated if a battalion suffered heavy losses during an attack.

One of these new "pals" battalions was the 16th Northumberland Fusiliers. They were called the Newcastle Commercials as they had been recruited from the city's professional classes.

A number of these new battalions[6] from Newcastle and South-East Northumberland wanted to be affiliated to Scottish and Irish regiments, calling themselves the Tyneside Scottish and Irish respectively. This was, however, refused by the War Office. The new battalions eventually agreed to become attached to the Northumberland Fusiliers but they were granted certain privileges such as having a pipe band[7]. There would be eight battalions[8] altogether, with a number of reserve battalions.

9: A postcard showing part of the Alnwick Camp.

The Duke of Northumberland made land available for a training camp on the Pastures near Alnwick Castle [9 & 10]. It was originally envisaged that this camp would be for three battalions: The Commercials, Tyneside Scottish and Tyneside

---

[6] Many of the pals battalions were initially funded by businessmen and other wealthy individuals; they could be considered "private armies". The Tyneside Scottish, for example, were only finally adopted by the War Office in August 1915.

[7] The Tyneside Scottish were also allowed to wear the glengarry cap.

[8] The 20th, 21st, 22nd and 23rd NF were called the 1st, 2nd, 3rd and 4th Tyneside Scottish respectively. The 24th, 25th, 26th and 27th NF were called the 1st, 2nd, 3rd and 4th Tyneside Irish.

Irish. In fact, so successful was the recruitment in the North-East, the camp would be expanded and would eventually accommodate the whole of the Tyneside Scottish Brigade; a body of over 4,000 men.

As early as 19th September 1914, the A&C Gazette was announcing:

> It is reported that a few thousand of men are to be quartered on ground in the Pasture north of the Havens, and the labour advertised for is required to construct huts for the accommodation of the troops. Many tons of timber have arrived at Alnwick Railway Station, presumably for the carrying out of this work. Gas for lighting and cooking is to be laid on.

10: A view of some of the huts at the Alnwick camp, showing how they were built on steeply sloping land

By October work had started, with up to 400 men being employed. One of the first tasks was the construction of a road from Denwick Lane to the old North Road near St Leonard's Hospital [8].

The work on the camp was supposed to be complete by November 1914 but there were repeated delays. This led to the Pioneer Sections of some battalions being sent to help the contractors get the camp finished.

The Newcastle Commercials started to occupy the site from 8th December 1914. They left Alnwick on 21st April 1915 to go to a new camp at Cramlington. They were in France by November 1915, serving as part of the 32nd Division.

The 1st Tyneside Scottish were the next to arrive, marching from Newcastle. They did this over a period two days, 29th and 30th January 1915, resting overnight at Morpeth. On their arrival at Alnwick they were welcomed by the band of the 16th Battalion and by the people of the town.

On the 12th March both the 2nd Tyneside Scottish and the 1st Tyneside Irish departed for Alnwick. The Irish arrived the same day; they went by train [11]. The Scottish marched, arriving the next day.

The Tyneside Irish arrive at Alnwick.

Photo]   [J. H. Sanderson.
Scene in Bondgate, Friday, March 12th.

11: The arrival of the 1st Tyneside Irish in Alnwick, passing what is now the Halifax and Lloyds Bank

The 1st Tyneside Irish didn't stay very long; they left Alnwick on 30th April 1915 to join with the other three Tyneside Irish battalions at a camp near Woolsington, where they formed the 103rd (Tyneside Irish)Brigade.

Finally, the 4th Tyneside Scottish moved to Alnwick on 29th April, and the 3rd Tyneside Scottish on 30th April.

The four Tyneside Scottish battalions were now together, completing the 102nd (Tyneside Scottish) Brigade. The men began to make themselves at home. Their huts soon acquired names, often those of the pubs in the villages where they came from.

The main purpose of the camp was training. The men would march for over 20 miles in the surrounding countryside, building up strength and stamina.

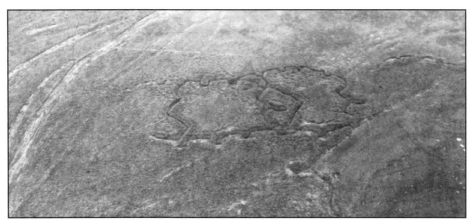

12: An aerial view of the practice trenches near Rothbury (OS map reference NU049034)

Trench building was a critical element in preparing soldiers for the Western Front, and it is probable that there were some practice trenches in the immediate surroundings. No remains are currently known, however, but there is a good example near Rothbury, which is on open access land and can still be visited today [12].

There were ranges for rifle practice. Two were already in existence on Alnwick Moor and two new ones were created on the Pastures themselves. Significant remains of the target butts at Moorlaws can still be seen [6]. There are also faint traces on Alnwick Moor (OS map reference NU166134).

Sports would also be a major feature of camp life, with inter-battalion football and boxing competitions. Sports days were popular and included intriguing events such as "pipers' 100 yard race" and "buglers' race" where the instruments had to be played while running! There were also cricket and football matches against teams from the town.

As well as the serious business of training and parading, there was also time for entertainment. Regular concerts were held in the camp and the A&C Gazette had a weekly review of life in the camp in its Hut Camp News. This section of the newspaper proved popular with the soldiers as they could send a cutting home to keep their families in touch with what was happening in the camp.

13: A postcard showing the inspection of the Tyneside Scottish by the Duke of Northumberland on the Pastures

On 18th May 1915 there was a major parade in the Pastures, where the brigade was inspected by the Duke of Northumberland [13]. Two days later the whole brigade went to Newcastle by train for the Kings Review on the Town Moor, where they were among over 18,000 soldiers who paraded in front of King George V and Lord Kitchener. It took a total of ten trains to move the soldiers to and from Newcastle!

The soldiers in the camp had ample opportunities to visit the town. A rest centre was established in the Northumberland Hall, where the men could get a cup of tea and socialise. Local shop keepers seized the opportunity to sell souvenirs. The local paper carried the following advertisement on 7th August 1915:

> *Tyneside Scottish! For Kilty Ties see AR Smith's window, Bondgate Hill; A memento for Lady Friends. Specially made for The Scottish, with brooch, name*

Also photographers from far afield descended on Alnwick, making postcards of the camp and its events for sale to the soldiers.

In mid-August, according to the A&C Gazette, the Tyneside Scottish left by train for a camp "somewhere in the south", returning a week later "harder than hammers".[9]

14: A postcard showing the 7th NF marching along the Alnwick Moor road towards their camp at Moorlaws

But the training did come to an end, and the Tyneside Scottish Brigade started to leave Alnwick during the latter part of August, to go to Salisbury Plain where they joined with the 101st and 103rd Brigades to form the 34th Division[10].

---

[9] "Harder Than Hammers" was the motto of the Tyneside Scottish
[10] Some sources have the Tyneside Scottish Brigade leaving Alnwick at the beginning of August.

The 34th Division was in France in January 1916, where they fought at La Boiselle on the opening day of the Battle of the Somme on 1st July 1916. They suffered terrible losses as they had to start their advance further back in order to avoid the expected debris from the planned detonation of the Lochnagar crater.

While the Tyneside Scottish were occupying the camp, companies from the 7th NF were still living in and around Alnwick. They were at times living in billets, but also spent time under canvas, including a camp at Moorlaws, on Alnwick moor [14].

There would ultimately be three battalions of the 7th. These were designated the 1st/7th, 2nd/7th and 3rd/7th. The 2nd/7th would spend some time in the Middle East, while the 3rd/7th were a reserve battalion.

The local paper reported on 11th September 1915 that:

The 3rd Line of this [3rd/7th] Battalion which is at present under canvas contemplates a route march next week with the Regimental Band in a part of the county little frequented by soldiers. The object of course is to get recruits to complete its strength, which is already diminished by drafts for overseas.

After the departure of the main body of the Tyneside Scottish, the camp started to be converted to a military convalescent hospital. The refurbishment took longer than expected, however, and it wasn't until January 1916 that patients began to arrive.

The camp took on a new appearance. The A&C Gazette reported on 8th April 1916:

A visit to the encampment in the Pastures this week, after an absence of a fortnight, revealed a wonderful change in the ornamental approaches to B and C camps. The shrubbery adorning the sides is flourishing beautifully through the dry weather of last week[11].

The convalescent hospitals were intended to receive injured soldiers who were expected to return to the front after six weeks treatment, which included:

---

[11] It has been reported that flowers were still blooming in the area of the camp for many years, until the use of herbicides became more common.

the dowsing heat treatment, and some 123 men are massaged every morning, while 70 others are being attended to by the ladies of the V.A.D., who dress their wounds.

The hospital also included two huts which were converted into a VAD hospital, administered by the Red Cross. This was occupied from 5th April 1916, at which time the hospital in Bailiffgate was closed.

By November 1916 the convalescent hospital had been closed and the camp was then used as a Command Depot for the rehabilitation of soldiers who were too fit for a convalescent camp, but not yet fit enough to be returned to their units. This new camp housed about 5,000 men from the Machine Gun Corps and Northern Command.

Throughout its life as a hospital, entertainment was a significant activity, with concerts every week. The highlight, however, was probably the visit of famous Scottish singer, Harry Lauder, in August 1916.

The final military use of the camp was by the Royal Naval Division, who occupied the camp at the end of the war and were demobilised from there. There are stories of the victory parade where the RND were a little worse for drink. They stopped the parade by the brewery to give three cheers and were so disruptive during the dignitaries' speeches that the event had to be curtailed!

At the end of the war the camp was abandoned. It had a brief revival, when some of the huts were occupied for a few days by about 400 fisher girls who had been stranded at Alnmouth station during the 1919 rail strike. They had been travelling south, following the herring fleets, and were able to resume their journey once the strike ended.

The huts within the camp were then auctioned and were used across the local area . Some were relocated to the Freemen's land on Alnwick Moor. The last of these huts was finally destroyed only a few years ago.

Nothing of significance now remains at the site of the camp[12].

---

[12] Northumberland Estates are currently allowing permissive access to much of the Pastures and so the area can be visited. The prevailing access arrangements are displayed at the main entrances which are adjacent to both the Denwick and Lion bridges.

Attacks from the Air

On the 16th December 1914 the German Navy bombarded a number of towns on the Yorkshire coast, including Whitby, Scarborough and Hartlepool. Over 130 people were killed in this one attack. Other naval bombardments followed. For the first time, the civilian population of Britain was being targeted in a seemingly indiscriminate manner. There was, unsurprisingly, a feeling of outrage and fear within the country.

On 28th December, the Chief Constable of Northumberland, Fullarton James, sent a memo to all Special Constables who lived within three miles of the coast.

> *After the event at Hartlepool it is only proper that instructions should be issued to you how to act in case a similar attack be experienced by your Town or District: you will understand that I am only talking of a bombardment, which would probably be over in 45 minutes or an hour. In this order I am not alluding to an attempted invasion.*

> *The experience of the Hartlepools shows that the best chance of safety lies in the people remaining in their own houses and not going out into the streets. Should there be any cellar, that would be the best place, otherwise the basement and the back whichever side is furthest from the enemy's guns.*

> *Your duty therefore, in the event of a bombardment, will be to wait for no further orders but immediately to act in the district surrounding your own dwelling, or where you may be at the time, by using all your efforts towards keeping the inhabitants off the streets and generally in inducing them to carry out the suggestions contained in paragraph 2.*

> *When the firing has ceased you will thoroughly visit the area for which you are acting and remove to hospital those who are injured, being careful to see that a building which has been hit and damaged has not buried in its ruins any human beings requiring help. Fires would also probably have broken out and would require immediate attention.*

In fact there were no naval bombardments that would affect Northumberland. In January 1915, however, the German Navy started to target Britain's civilian

NOTICE.

PRECAUTIONS to be observed by the Inhabitants in the possible Event of

ATTACK BY AIRCRAFT.

1.—On the 31st December it was thought necessary to issue a Proclamation dealing with the possible bombardment of the Coast of this County by the Enemy's Fleet, and recent events show that the further question of an attack by Aircraft should be provided against beforehand.

2.—Several of the points mentioned in the Proclamation of the 31st December, apply to an Aircraft attack, as for example:—

(a). The avoidance of people crowding together;

(b). The great desirability of all persons remaining in their houses and not running out to the streets; further

(c). If an enemy Aircraft is seen or heard overhead, crowds should disperse, and all persons should, if possible, take shelter: the effects of a bomb falling on soft ground—ploughed fields, etc.—are usually small and local.

(d). Unexploded bombs should not be touched as they may burst if moved: the local Police or Military Authorities should be informed where they are, as soon as this can be done safely.

3.—LIGHTS: Arrangements have now been made throughout the whole of Northumberland, by which, should any warning of the approach of enemy Aircraft at night be received, all the Town Lighting (and outside the area served by the Newcastle and Gateshead Gas Company—all the Private Lighting as well) will be turned off. This would necessarily be done without the possibility of communicating with the inhabitants. [This Paragraph refers to Gas and Electric Lighting.]

4.—Should the measures referred to in the above paragraph have to be taken, Inhabitants are warned:—

(a). To immediately turn off the gas at their meters and gas cocks to prevent escape of gas when the gas supply is again turned on;

(b). To provide themselves with Candles or Lamps as the gas almost certainly, and the electric light probably, will not be turned on again till the following morning.

5.—The possibility of outbreaks of Fire in such emergencies must be provided for by the Brigades throughout the County.

6.—The County Constabulary and Special Constables have already received their orders and it is most desirable that the inhabitants carry out any instructions that may be received from them.

NORTHUMBERLAND,
LORD-LIEUTENANT.

29th January, 1915.

15: A poster issued by the Duke of Northumberland giving the precautions necessary in case of air from the air

population with bombs dropped from Zeppelin airships. In Northumberland there was an immediate response, with a poster being issued that gave detailed instructions to the local population [15].

16: A postcard showing a Zeppelin over Blyth. These cards were very popular at the time but were normally forgeries; the Zeppelin raids tended to be at night. Also the people in the picture do not seem overly concerned with the airship looming behind them!

On the night of 2nd April 1916, Zeppelin L16 crossed the coast near Cresswell and dropped over forty bombs as it traversed the county. It finally headed out to sea over Coquet Island. The A&C Gazette reported:

The north-east coast was visited with another air raid on Sunday night, further north than any yet exploited. In one district a few miles inland the first public intimation given that the hostile aircraft were expected in the district was the shutting off of the gas and electric lights[13], and police and

---

[13] In the camp in the Pastures there were problems when the lights went out. Some men were in town and found it hard to get back in the dark, many ending up in the wrong parts of the camp.

special constables afterwards took especially prompt initiatives, doing valuable work in warning people and seeing that their lights were out.

About twenty minutes before and twenty minutes after midnight the district was visited by an enemy air ship which dropped about twenty bombs, four or five near to a country mansion, but no damage was done other than destroying a large part of the field.

The reports of the exploding bombs were heard for several miles away, the night being calm and starlit. For a distance of twelve miles around, the windows of the houses were shaken in their frames, crowds of people, many being disturbed from their slumbers, turned out alarmed, but there was no indication of any panic, possibly because of the bomb dropping being several miles off.

A good number sought the higher grounds commanding a view of the sea, and from these points of vantage the flashes of the exploding bombs were plainly seen, and even the sound of the engines of the aircraft could be heard. There are no reports of any serious damage to property or loss of life or injury, and it is supposed that the district in question was only visited by one Zeppelin which was not observed. At 12.20 the last bomb was heard and at 12.30 the special constables were discharged.

The prevailing air of secrecy is clear from the lack of local detail within this report, which is a little surprising as it was likely to be common knowledge within the locality.

The April air raid was followed by another on the night of 2nd May when Zeppelin L11 crossed the coast near Lindisfarne and flew south before heading out to sea near Amble. Only two bombs were dropped.

Finally, on the night of 9th August Zeppelin L14 crossed the coast at Berwick and flew westward to Kelso before heading out to sea at Alnmouth early the next morning. All the bombs fell in open countryside.

None of these raids caused any loss of life nor very much damage to property, though a report in the A&C Gazette stated that during the April raid:

the ceiling in a cottage came down and a pheasant was killed.

The lack of success of these raids was probably mainly due to the difficulties of navigation during the darkness; the slow moving air ships needed the protection of the night. In fact it is quite likely that the raids were intended to target the industrial areas further south, around the Tyne and Tees.

The air attacks, however, led to the local deployment of aircraft of the Royal Flying Corps. On 18th March 1916, 36 (Home Defence) Squadron was formed at Cramlington. In October 1916, it was divided into three separate flights which would each operate from different airfields. C flight moved to a new airfield that had been built at Ashington. They also made use of a number of support landing fields around the county, of which there were three in the Alnwick area.

The first landing field was opened in October 1916 near Rennington, but this was closed in February 1917; we can assume that there must have been some problem with it. Another landing field was opened nearby at Stamford in December 1916 which remained open until June 1919. There was a third landing field near Snipe House, to the south of Alnwick, which operated between March 1917 and June 1919.

After the Zeppelin raids in 1916, there were no further air raids in the Alnwick area but, despite this, the blackout was strictly maintained. The local paper regularly reported the fines for people who had inadvertently been showing lights at night.

In May 1917 the Germans started using bomber aircraft to raid England. The success of these attacks prompted the Duke of Northumberland to issue the following guidance on 14th August 1917. It was directed to everyone who lived in the county.

After 3 years of war it may be advisable to remind the inhabitants of Northumberland that in the event of any enemy attack, whether from the air or sea, the best chance of security lies in immediately taking cover.

The recent day attacks in the South of England have proved that, as a rule persons who take cover find security, while those that remain in the open are in far greater danger.

In this connection it must be borne in mind that the risk is not only from bombs dropped by hostile aircraft but also from falling shell splinters from our own anti-aircraft guns and from bullets from machine guns fired during an aerial encounter; also from falling houses and debris.

In fact, there were no bomber raids in the north of the country; the range of the aircraft would not be enough for such a flight.

Although there were no more raids, regular air patrols continued throughout the remainder of the war. Much of the flying would have been done at night. At this time night flying would have been a specialised skill, which led to 36 Squadron taking on a night flying training role for new pilots.

In April 1918, just before the end of the war, the Royal Air Force came into being as a separate service, created by a merger of the Army's Royal Flying Corps and the Navy's Royal Naval Air Service. This recognised the increased role that aircraft had made during the past four years and the need for strategic planning for this new form of warfare.

At the end of the war all the landing fields around Alnwick were closed down and nothing remains to be seen today.

17: A BE2 aircraft, as used by 36 Squadron for night flying. This was a stable machine, no longer suited to the rigours of the Western Front, but ideal for night flying against the threat of Zeppelins.

The Aftermath

The Great War marked a watershed in British social history. It has been said that modern Britain was born in 1918.

Even before the end of the war, all men over 21 years had been given the vote, together with most women over 30 years. The electorate increased threefold, totally changing the face of politics.

Technology was given a massive push forward. In 1914, the sight of an aeroplane would merit a mention in the local paper. By 1918 they had become a common sight in the area. Similarly, motor cars, which were rare in 1914, would become increasingly common on the roads, as would the cheaper alternative of motor bike and sidecar.

During the war, women had stepped into many roles traditionally done by men. After the war, this change would not be reversed and women would become an increasing presence in all areas of business.

Some of the most lasting legacies of the war are perhaps the memorials that were established in every town and village across the country where the names of all those in the Armed Forces who have have died during conflicts are still recorded.

Locally we have many war memorials in Alnwick and the surrounding villages, as well as in churches and other public buildings. There are also a number of graves in local cemeteries and church yards for soldiers of the Great War [7].

As well as the memorials to the dead, in the Northumberland Hall there is a roll of honour, listing 1200 men from Alnwick who served in the war. There is also a bench by the Alnwick war memorial which is dedicated to "the brave men and women of Alnwick who served their country in the Great War 1914-1918".

The Great War has sometimes been portrayed as a tragic mistake that led to the loss of so many lives. While all war is a tragedy, we should not forget that the men who died did so protecting the liberty that we all benefit from today. Without Britain's intervention in the conflict, it is quite likely that Germany would have prevailed and dominated mainland Europe for many years.

Bibliography and Further Reading

Relics of War, A Guide to the 20th Century Military Remains in the Northumberland Landscape; Hall I, Wanney Books 2013

Weekend Warriors, From Tyne to Tweed; Hewitson TL, Tempus 2006

Tyneside Scottish, 20th, 21st, 22nd & 23rd (Service) Battalions of the Northumberland Fusiliers; Stewart G, Sheen J, Pen and Sword Books 1999

Action Stations, Military Airfields of Scotland, the North-East and Northern Ireland; Smith D, Patrick Stephens 1983

North East Aviation Diary, Aviation Incidents from 1790 - 1999; D Walton, Norav Publications 1999

Acknowledgements

I would like to thank the following people for their invaluable assistance in creating this book:

All the members of the Alnwick District WW1 Centenary Commemoration Group for their help in getting this book finalised; Derek Gladding, Jane Glass, Mo Dewar, David Thompson, Neil Brison, Dave Barras, Bill Foote and Neil Tonge.

David Easton, who initially got me involved in the whole project.

Keith Barron, who returned the papers relating to the invasion precautions to the area: the WFA will be making a donation to the RNLI in recognition of this.

Clifford Pettit for all his help, particularly regarding the Army in Alnwick, and for the use of his photographs.

Barry Mead for the history of 36 Squadron.

Phil Rowett for the Zeppelin photograph.

All the folks at Azure for their help in printing the book.

And finally, the ladies in Alnwick library who always were welcoming whenever I went in to search the Alnwick and County Gazette microfiche records.

Supporting Organisations

The Western Front Association

Nationally, the WFA was formed with the aim of furthering interest in the Great War of 1914-1918. It also aims to perpetuate the memory, courage and comradeship of all those, on all sides, who served their countries in France and Flanders and their own countries during the Great War. Established in 1980 by noted military historian John Giles, the WFA has grown over the years to some 6,000 members worldwide.

The North Northumberland Branch of the Western Front Association (WFA) meets on the fourth Monday of every month (except August and December) at Alnmouth and District Ex-Servicemen's Club and Institute, Northumberland Street, Alnmouth. If you would like to learn more, please visit the WFA's website:

www.westernfrontassociation.com.

Alnwick District WW1 Centenary Commemoration Group

This is a recently constituted group, drawn from a range of volunteers including local members of the WFA and Royal British Legion. The objects of the group are to mark the centenary of WW1 with a series of projects and events, and to build a fitting and lasting legacy to honour the response to the nation's call to arms.

If you would like to learn more, please visit the Group's website:

www.bailiffgatemuseum.co.uk/WW1

All profits from the sale of this book, including those of the author and the publisher, will go to supporting the work of the local WFA and the Alnwick District WW1 Centenary Commemoration Group.